# SYDNEY
## AUSTRALIA

*Steve Parish*

THE SIGNATURE COLLECTION

Page 1: Sydney Opera House and Sydney Harbour Bridge.

Above: The cruise ship Oriana is escorted from the Heads to Circular Quay.

*Sydney's first surf lifesaving club was founded in 1906. Today, surf lifesaving carnivals showcase traditional surf rescue skills. Above, a surfboat crew battles the waves.*

*Sydney Harbour, Opera House and Harbour Bridge — the magnificent combination of natural beauty and high human endeavour that makes Sydney one of the world's great cities.*

# CONTENTS

Busy George Street runs through The Rocks to end at Dawes Point, near the Harbour Bridge.

The Rocks, the site of original settlement in 1788, is a fascinating place to visit.

## SYDNEY, MAGNIFICENCE ON A SPARKLING HARBOUR

There are many ways to arrive in Sydney.

You can step off a jetplane, or walk down the gangplank of a cruise liner, or jump ashore from an ocean-going yacht. You can whirl into the city in a train, or whirr down in a helicopter, or dismount from a bicycle, or even descend from a balloon. However, most people arrive by air or by road, and either mode of transport gives a wonderful preview of Australia's oldest and largest city.

If weather, pilot and air traffic controllers are kind, a flypast allows a magnificent view of Sydney Harbour and its icons, the Bridge and the Opera House. Arrival by road across the Harbour Bridge allows more intimate views of sparkling water dotted with myriad craft, the gorgeous curves of the Opera House, and a panorama of Australia's greatest city.

Half the population of the State of New South Wales live in Sydney – nearly four million vibrant bodies. This is just under one-quarter of Australia's total. Yet the city preserves its natural beauties, prime among them the Harbour and its contributing rivers, the ocean beaches, a multitude of parks and public gardens, and suburbs alive with green trees and colourful flowers. This wonderful setting is complemented by national parks to south and north, the Blue Mountains to the west and, to the east, the blue Pacific Ocean.

The city itself is full of architectural gems: some dating from the early 1800s, others as new as tomorrow. Sydneysiders have a "can do" approach to construction, as witness the splendid complexes raised to house the Year 2000 Olympics. In the city, older buildings pay tribute to European conventions, while more modern ones take full advantage of a marvellous climate that encourages all-year-round outdoor pleasures.

Multicultural and full of vigorous cultural and sporting activities, a great place to dine and see the sights, a vital business centre with immediate links to the rest of the world, Sydney is unique in its blend of the cosmopolitan with the truly Australian. It's a great place to visit and an even better place to live.

I love it!

*Steve Parish*

*The view south-east over Sydney Harbour to the Pacific Ocean is stunning. The mighty Harbour Bridge links the north shore to the city, Opera House and beyond.*

*Sydney Harbour Bridge seen at dusk from Dawes Point. Known affectionately as "the coathanger", the Bridge was opened in 1932. Sixteen lives were lost in its construction.*

*Looking across Kirribilli and Sydney Harbour to (from left) the Royal Botanic Gardens, Sydney Opera House, Circular Quay, The Rocks and Sydney Harbour Bridge.*

*Sydney city skyline and freeway, viewed from the Cahill Expressway. The city centre is compact and bordered by Circular Quay, Darling Harbour and the Royal Botanic Gardens.*

## SYDNEY AT NIGHT

Sydney's Central Business District is compact, despite a building boom that keeps splendid new buildings raising their towers above the gracious relicts of colonial times. After dark, there's plenty to do and see in the city and neighbouring areas such as Kings Cross, Darlinghurst and Paddington.

At night, Sydney promises, and delivers, fun, frolic and great food. As the lights come on, the restaurants open and theatres light up. Take your choice of entertainment, from classical drama, ballet, opera and music to the latest films and stage extravaganzas. There are plenty of jazz clubs, alternative cafes and nightclubs. It's a great place to party.

*At night, Sydney CBD resembles a gemstone display case of diamonds, rubies and topaz.*
*This view, which includes Sydney Tower (left) is from the old Pyrmont Bridge.*

*Looking south-west from Milsons Point across Sydney Harbour to the business heart of the city. Sydney Harbour Bridge is at the right of the picture.*

## THE SYDNEY TOWER AND THE MONORAIL

The Sydney Tower's 30-m spire is 305 metres above street level, and the tower itself is the tallest construction in the Southern Hemisphere. The nine-level turret can hold 1000 people, and contains an observation level, cafes and restaurants. The tower was opened in 1981. It is held steady in even the strongest winds by two sets of 56 cables, each weighing 7 tonnes. Each of its lifts takes only 40 seconds to pass 76 floors on the way to the Observation Level, or the climb can be done the hard way – plodding up 1474 steps on one of the two stairways to the top.

The Monorail whisks silently around the inner city, passing through the city centre, Chinatown and Darling Harbour. The entire circuit takes 12 minutes. Cars leave every few minutes and stop at each of seven stations.

*Sydney Tower and surrounding buildings silhouetted against the glow of dusk.*

*Golden Sydney Tower stands proud against an azure sky. In the foreground, a Monorail car turns into Market Street on its route to Darling Harbour.*

*The clock that dominates the interior of the QVB chimes on the hour. The building contains many mementos of the Victorian era and is guarded by a statue of the Good Queen.*

## THE QUEEN VICTORIA BUILDING

Visiting the Queen Victoria Building is like meeting a venerable lady who, as if by magic, has been restored to the full splendour of her youth. This historic edifice, one of Sydney's great shrines for serious shoppers, stands on ground set aside for a marketplace by Governor Macquarie in 1810. In 1828, the area became a police court, in 1869 a roofed market and in 1893 a splendid edifice named the Queen Victoria Markets Building. Today, restored and rejuvenated, the QVB epitomises the grandiose style of late Victorian architecture and its five levels house many of Sydney's most prestigious boutiques, stylish cafes and fashionable salons.

*Top: The QVB occupies a whole city block. Here, the central dome glows at night.*

*Above: Stained glass windows are a feature of the Queen Victoria Building.*

## SHOPPING IN SYDNEY

For serious shoppers, Sydney's centre is the place to find both bargains and exclusive goods. In recent years many brand-name shops have opened branches in the city. Pedestrians roam the numerous shopping arcades lining Pitt Street Mall and are enticed into busy department stores. Nearby, Queen Victoria Building has been transformed into a fascinating shopping venue to rival the classic Victorian-era Strand Arcade between Pitt and George Streets. Retail centres such as Centrepoint, Skygarden and the Glasshouse can also be found in Pitt Street Mall, along with hundreds of specialty shops.

Further downtown, The Rocks, with its cobbled laneways restored, caters for tourists. Darling Harbour, a convention, exhibition and shopping centre on the waterfront just to the west of the city centre, is another shoppers' mecca. Close to the city, excellent shopping precincts full of specialty stores abound in suburbs such as Double Bay, Paddington, Woollahra, Glebe, Newtown and Chatswood.

*Pitt Street Mall, in the centre of Sydney, is a popular place for people to promenade, shop, eat and just sit around watching the lunchtime crowd.*

*Strand Arcade runs between Pitt Street and George Street. It is shopping paradise for the discriminating, and a showplace, with its tiled floors, iron balustrades and glass roof.*

*Top to bottom: Creperie Stivell, Paddington; The Tea Centre of Sydney, Paddington; The Country Trader, Paddington; Queen Street Fruit Market, Woollahra.*

*Top: DeCosti Seafoods, Sydney Fish Markets, Pyrmont, an outlet for fabulously fresh seafood.*

*Above: Orson and Blake Collectables, Queen Street, Woollahra.*

The Sydney Opera House on Bennelong Point, seen over Sydney Cove. The sails, as the shells of the curved roofs are called, rise some 70 metres above the Harbour.

## THE SYDNEY OPERA HOUSE

The Sydney Opera house is located on Bennelong Point to the east of Circular Quay. A series of theatres and halls sheltered by curving, shell-like roofs, it is one of the world's most memorable public buildings. Designed in 1956 by the Danish architect Jorn Utzon, the building was not completed until 1973, after a series of disputes that saw Utzon resign and the project brought to completion by a team of local architects. The Opera House is actually a venue for live theatre, opera, ballet, modern dance and classical music. Its sight-seeing tours are almost as popular as its performances and various sections are used for fashion parades and other crowd-pleasing activities.

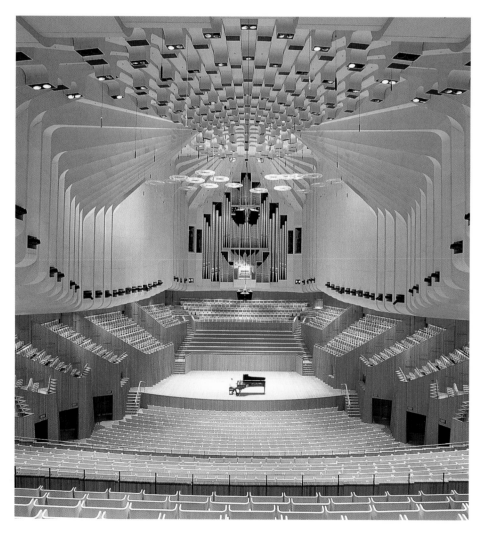

*A pianist rehearsing in the Concert Hall, Sydney Opera House. The Concert Hall seats 2690 and is used for all kinds of music as well as opera and dance.*

*Utzon visualised the Opera House as a "living sculpture" to be seen from land, sea or air.*

*The shell-like framework was modelled on the spreading ribs of a palm leaf.*

*Sydney Opera House at dusk, as seen from Circular Quay.*

## THE ROYAL BOTANIC GARDENS

The present Royal Botanic Gardens and the adjoining Domain are full of memories of convict and colonial times. The area was the site of the colony's first farm and also of its first public park. Nearby Macquarie Street is home to some of Australia's oldest public buildings, as well as Parliament House. The Domain is a green space in two parts, used variously as a public forum, a place for exercise and picnicking, and an outdoor theatre. It is a place where outdoor concerts and opera can be enjoyed, especially in January during the Festival of Sydney.

*The Domain peninsula juts into the Harbour. At the end is a rock formation called Mrs Macquaries Chair where the wife of the famous governor used to sit and admire the water.*

*Symbols, icons and useful as well – Sydney Opera House and Sydney Harbour Bridge viewed from Mrs Macquaries Point on the Domain peninsula of the Royal Botanic Gardens.*

*In a city where modern development has taken the form of towers (top left), the sedate low-rise buildings of The Rocks offer a taste of the nineteenth century.*

## THE ROCKS: HISTORIC AND CONTEMPORARY

A short walk from Circular Quay, within the aura of the Harbour Bridge, is The Rocks, site of the first European settlement in Australia. In 1788 convicts from the First Fleet cleared the area that gained the name "The Rocks" because of its sandstone outcrops. Today, thanks to conservationists who rejected a plan that would have seen the area levelled for high-rise development, many of the buildings have been restored. Pubs and restaurants mingle with art and craft galleries, boutiques, specialty and gift shops full of Australian products. There is a fine Museum of Contemporary Arts and, at weekends, a well-patronised market offering all sorts of art and craftwork.

*Top: The Lord Nelson in The Rocks is said to be Sydney's oldest pub.*

*Above: Cadman's Cottage, Sydney's oldest surviving house, was built in 1816.*

## SYDNEY'S GRACIOUS BUILDINGS

The gold rushes of the mid-1800s and a continuing demand for wool for the mills of England brought prosperity to New South Wales and some splendid buildings to its capital. Many are constructed of the warm golden sandstone characteristic of the Sydney area.

The Art Gallery of New South Wales was established in 1874 and moved into its stately classical home in 1897. It displays collections of Australian and overseas art, including one of the world's finest collections of Aboriginal and Torres Strait Islander works.

*The Art Gallery of New South Wales houses paintings, prints, drawings and photographs by Australian, European and Asian artists, and the Yiribana Gallery of indigenous art and culture.*

Governor Macquarie laid the foundation stone for St Mary's Cathedral in 1821 on the first
land granted to the Catholic Church in Australia. The cathedral was consecrated in 1882.

## CIRCULAR QUAY, SYDNEY'S CENTRE

Circular Quay on the shores of Sydney Cove is the place where, on 26 January 1788, the colony of New South Wales was declared. Today it is the main city terminus for ferries, buses and trains, and the embarkation point for harbour cruises. It is also the place where Sydneysiders gather to celebrate New Year and other happenings. The area between the Quay and The Rocks offers waterside open space, top restaurants and an excellent place to enjoy the Harbour's nautical scene. The promenade from there around to the Opera House and the Botanic Gardens showcases all that makes Sydney such a special city.

*Sculptures on Circular Quay. Nearby, Writers Walk is set with pavement plaques noting the views of famous writers, Australian and otherwise, about "The Land Down Under".*

*The walkway around Circular Quay leading to the Overseas Passenger Terminal, Sydney Cove, with the Bridge in the background.*

*The replica of Bligh's famous ship, HMS Bounty, moored at Campbells Cove,*

*with the Opera House in the background.*

## THE HMAV BOUNTY

Built for the movie *The Bounty* that starred Mel Gibson, Sydney's HMAV *Bounty* is an exact-size, fully-rigged replica of the original vessel whose crew mutinied against Captain William Bligh in 1789. The vessel is 42 metres long and weighs 400 tonnes; its three masts are made from British Columbian pine with the main one 40 metres tall. The ship participated in the First Fleet re-enactment in 1988, and the following year was sailed to the South Pacific to re-enact the 200-year anniversary of the original mutiny. Today, HMAV *Bounty* is berthed at historic Campbells Cove at The Rocks. Her concessions to modernity are all below deck and include twin turbo-charged marine diesel engines. The *Bounty* sails Sydney Harbour throughout the year, giving locals and visitors alike a taste of eighteenth-century adventure cushioned by twentieth-century facilities and cuisine.

*HMAV **Bounty** is a splendid sight as it cruises Sydney Harbour, taking enthralled sailors-for-a-day on a voyage they will long remember.*

*Sydney is a working port, and the Overseas Passenger Terminal is within a stone's throw of the Harbour Bridge. Here, a luxury liner's lights compete with the brilliance of the city.*

## THE SYDNEY HARBOUR BRIDGE

Sydney Harbour Bridge was considered a considerable engineering feat when it was completed in 1932. Spanning the harbour for over 500 metres between Dawes Point at The Rocks and Milsons Point at North Sydney, its deck is 49 metres wide and 59 metres above the harbour. The massive steel structure carries more than 15 000 vehicles per hour during peak times. The south-eastern pylon is open for sightseers, while the bridge itself is accessible from The Rocks to pedestrians who wish to walk across the harbour. Some daring souls take part in bridge-top climbs, during which they have a unique view of city, harbour and beyond from 134 metres above the water.

*Sydney Harbour Bridge seen from the café on the deck of Sydney Opera House.*

# DARLING HARBOUR

Darling Harbour, just to the west of the city centre, is the place to go for shopping and dining. Once dilapidated railway goods yards and dockland, the redeveloped area was opened in 1988. It is now a weekend destination for thousands of people who flock to the exhibition, convention and shopping complexes, as well as to the Chinese Gardens and tree-lined walkways. Nearby, the Sydney Aquarium, National Maritime Museum, Motor Museum and Powerhouse Museum are major attractions. The old Pyrmont Bridge, now a pedestrian walkway, links the city with this fascinating precinct.

*Top and above: Darling Harbour is one of Sydney's most impressive precincts and an ideal place to relax or visit a multitude of features including museums and the Sydney Aquarium.*

*Darling Harbour, a premier Sydney attraction, can be reached by monorail, on foot across the old Pyrmont Bridge, by cruise vessel or by water taxi.*

*Cockle Bay Wharf complements the original Darling Harbour development. At the end of the walkway is the Panasonic IMAX Theatre.*

## COCKLE BAY WHARF, DARLING HARBOUR

Cockle Bay Wharf is a welcome addition to Darling Harbour's many attractions. This large complex, on Cockle Bay past the Pyrmont Bridge, is famous for its fabulous variety of restaurants and cafés. Dining experiences can be as simple or as extravagant as the visitor desires, and sitting by the waterside on a warm summer evening, eating fabulous seafood and watching the lights of the city, is sheer magic. The waters of Cockle Bay play host to spectacular film and laser shows enthralling audiences, while the nearby Panasonic IMAX Theatre boasts "the world's biggest movie screen".

*City buildings, notable among them the shining Sydney Tower, seen over Darling Harbour's Cockle Bay.*

*Top: One of Sydney Aquarium's most popular features, a walk-through tunnel.*

*Above: A view across Darling Harbour and Sydney Aquarium to the western side of the CBD.*

*The Chinese Garden of Friendship near Darling Harbour was built in 1987, its design a gift to Sydney from its sister city, Guangdong. It is a peaceful and beautiful place.*

Top: The entrance of the National Maritime Museum. The roof symbolises a wave, or the bows of a ship. Above: A display of maritime signal flags in front of the Maritime Museum.

# THE NATIONAL MARITIME MUSEUM, DARLING HARBOUR

Sydney's fascinating National Maritime Museum, at Darling Harbour, shows how closely Australians are linked to the sea. The exhibitions explore many maritime themes, including Aboriginal seafaring traditions. Displays cover European exploration of the South Pacific and Australia's coasts, naval life past and present, water sports and recreations. There are models of ships from the 1950s liner *Orcades* to the hydroplane *Spirit of Australia*, which in 1978 set a world water speed record of 511 km/h.

A special gallery recalls two centuries of maritime contact between the USA and Australia. Amongst the historic vessels moored at the museum's wharves are a Vietnamese refugee boat, the 1959 Australian Royal Navy destroyer *Vampire*, a navy patrol boat, a WWII commando raider and an array of working craft, including pearling and fishing boats.

*An aerial view of the National Maritime Museum.*

## AFTER DARK, THE CITY LIGHTS

After dark, Sydney is a city of light. Shops and signs flash and glow, office blocks sparkle, trees and gardens are softly illuminated and traffic scribbles brilliant ruby and gold through the streets. Best of all are the occasions when Sydneysiders do things in style and fireworks light sky and water with starbursts, comet-trails and novas of light. New Years Eve is the occasion of one of the best of these pyrotechnic displays, but there are plenty more – the harbour city is one of the best places ever to throw a party to which everyone is invited.

*Above left: A night view from Pyrmont Bridge towards the city centre.*

*Above right: New Years Eve, fireworks turn the Harbour into a fairyland.*

Top: Star City combines a host of attractions, including gaming, theatres, and a five-star hotel.

Above: The lights of the Harbourside Festival Marketplace seen across Cockle Bay.

## LOOKING WEST OF SYDNEY CITY

The Anzac Bridge is the gateway to Sydney's north-western suburbs. The roadway is suspended by lines of cables anchored to the tops of two massive concrete towers. The new structure, which offers fine views over the inner western suburbs and Blackwattle Bay, dwarfs the old opening bridge. Sydney's west is the growth region and new suburbs feed an urban sprawl stretching towards the Blue Mountains. Parramatta and Penrith have developed into important retail and commercial centres while, in the south-west, Liverpool and Campbelltown are cities in their own right.

*Anzac Bridge, seen from Rozelle Bay at dusk.*

*Travelling towards the city on Anzac Bridge. This links the north-western suburbs with the city centre and makes the "inland" route in and out of the city quick and efficient.*

*Opposite: Reflections of Sydney.*

*Above: Nineteenth-century Campbell's Storehouses (sandstone lower bays completed by 1861, brick upper story added 1890) and the city reflected.*

*An aerial view of Stadium Australia, venue for the opening and closing ceremonies of the XXVII Olympiad as well as for other premier sporting events.*

## OLYMPIC PARK, HOMEBUSH BAY

At Homebush Bay, 16 kilometres west of the city centre, stand the sports facilities for the Year 2000 Olympics. The most spectacular is Stadium Australia, which, with a crowd capacity of 110 000, is the largest of any outdoor Olympic stadium. A variety of other sporting venues stands nearby. The central location of the Olympic site means that it is also the perfect venue for concerts and a variety of sporting events. The complex is accessible by ferry via the Parramatta River, as well as by road and rail; the transport system's efficient design promises to shift even a capacity crowd with ease.

*Stadium Australia dominates the Homebush Bay Olympic site.*

*The Three Sisters, pillars of eroded sandstone, overlook the Jamison Valley. They are one of the Blue Mountains' most famous features.*

## THE BLUE MOUNTAINS

Two hours' drive (105 kilometres) west of Sydney and part of the Great Dividing Range, the Blue Mountains have been a holiday playground for Sydney since the advent of the railway in the mid 1800s. Towns perched on spectacular sandstone cliffs, including Leura, Springwood, Katoomba and Blackheath, offer a variety of accommodation, historic sites, beautiful gardens and galleries. The Three Sisters, Echo Point, Govetts Leap, Mount Tomah Botanic Gardens and Wentworth Falls are just a few of the mountains' attractions. Named for the blue haze caused by light reflecting from countless droplets of oil exhaled by eucalypt forests, the Blue Mountains is a haven for bushwalkers, birdwatchers, naturelovers and people seeking tranquillity and relaxation.

*Katoomba, one of the Blue Mountains' major centres, has a magnificent location on the edge of the scenic Jamison Valley.*

*Altitude gives the Blue Mountains an ideal climate for planting gardens such as this one in Mt Wilson, particularly lovely in spring and (above) autumn.*

*Top: Beauchamp Falls, one of the many spectacular waterfalls in the Blue Mountains.*

*Bottom: Koalas thrive on the abundant eucalypt leaves of the Blue Mountains.*

## SOUTH TO WOLLONGONG

The industrial city of Wollongong is around an hour's drive (80 kilometres) south of Sydney. Situated on the coastal plain between the brooding Illawarra Escarpment and the Pacific Ocean, it was from 1844 a port, loading coal and timber. Once, large stands of rainforest grew in the area. Much of it, especially the prized red cedar, was felled, but now there are only fragments left in the hidden valleys of the escarpment.

Today, Wollongong is a diverse and prosperous city with a highly regarded university, a regional gallery and fine botanic gardens. Its industrial title has been surrendered to its sister city of Port Kembla, site of a famous steelworks.

*The city of Wollongong, with the Illawarra Escarpment in the background. The harbour, in the centre of the picture, now provides moorings for pleasure craft and fishing vessels.*

*The spectacular coastline looking south from Sydney to Royal National Park and Wollongong. Semi Detached Point is in the foreground.*

*An aerial view over Sydney's eastern suburbs. They include Woolloomooloo, Rushcutters Bay and the prestige residential areas of Darling Point, Point Piper, Double Bay and Vaucluse.*

*An aerial view over The Gap and Watsons Bay and the eastern suburbs and Harbour to the city. The Opera House and Harbour Bridge are at the top right.*

*The El Alamein Fountain, a popular meeting place in "The Cross".*

## KINGS CROSS LIVE AT NIGHT

Once an area where artists, poets and novelists rubbed shoulders with theatre people, Kings Cross is still a place that really comes to life when the sun sets and the lights blaze on. "The Cross" is the most densely populated part of Sydney, home to restaurants, clubs and entertainment venues of all kinds. Hotels, boarding houses and backpackers' hostels offer accommodation for the many visitors who take advantage of the area's attractions, variety of hospitality and proximity to the city.

The Cross is part of the suburb of Potts Point, and many of its side streets are lined with beautiful old terrace houses and shady trees. It is a popular place to live as well as to play and to see the sights.

*Darlinghurst Road, lined with shops, cafés and restaurants, seldom closes.*

*Bondi Beach is popular with locals and visitors alike. On a fine summer's day it is crowded with swimmers, sunbakers and surfers. Winter brings beachwalkers and joggers onto the sand.*

## BONDI'S GOLDEN STRAND

The name Bondi needs no added "Beach" to bring international recognition. On a summer's day the famed "one thousand metres of golden sand" is packed with locals and visitors who come to sun themselves and plunge into the cool ocean waters. Shops and cafes line the boulevard that curves around the sandy crescent of the beach. A popular destination with backpackers from all over the world, Bondi and nearby Bondi Junction are cosmopolitan, densely populated residential suburbs with a strong European influence that is derived from post-war migration. This is the home of Australia's oldest surf lifesaving club, founded in 1906, and the finish of Sydney's annual City to Surf Fun-Run.

*Looking west over Dover Heights and Bondi Beach towards the city and Harbour (top right).*

*An aerial perspective of traditional lifesaving surfboats about to go into action. They are competing in a carnival at Bondi Beach.*

## SURF LIFESAVING – SNATCHING SOULS FROM THE SEA

Every Sydney ocean beach, and indeed every major Australian beach, has a surf lifesaving club. The clubs perform a very real service retrieving swimmers and surfers who have challenged the ocean and lost. Besides the reel and line and traditional surfboats, clubs now use modern rescue vessels and lifesaving techniques. However, the traditional surf rescue methods feature in surf carnivals. These provide stunning summertime displays which now include popular Ironman and Ironwoman contests between finely-honed athletes.

In recent times, women have taken their place in surf lifesaving teams and now account for one-third of their numbers.

*Curl Curl Surf Life Saving Club team in a march-past on carnival day.*

*With sails filling with wind, vessels make their way towards the Heads to begin the long and perilous Sydney to Hobart Yacht Race.*

## CHALLENGING WIND AND WAVES ON THE HARBOUR

On any day of the year "yachties" can be found navigating vessels of all shapes and sizes on the protected waters of Sydney Harbour. Taking best advantage of the prevailing winds, the zigzag patterns of tacking boats add an element of colourful chaos to harbour life. Australia's premier yachting event, the Sydney to Hobart Yacht Race, is held annually, starting on Boxing Day. Boats from all around the world gather in Sydney for the dash down Australia's south-east coast. The fastest yachts take a little over two and a half days to make the 1167 kilometre journey. Winners are awarded in both the handicap and line honours categories, but for many the thrill is in just participating and surviving a voyage which, if the weather turns nasty, can be perilous.

*Sydney Harbour is one of the best places in the world to be out on the water, challenging wind and waves with a crew of enthusiastic fellow sailors.*

*Boxing Day, and ocean-going yachts heel over as they pass Sydney's eastern suburbs, on the first leg of the long race to Constitution Dock, Hobart.*

*Looking south-east over Robertsons Point, Mosman Bay, Little Sirius Cove, Athol Bay, and Bradleys Head, to Rose Bay and finally to the Pacific Ocean.*

The elegant Elephant House is a feature of Taronga Park Zoo. The elephants have a fine view of Sydney Harbour and the city.

## TARONGA PARK, A ZOO WITH A VIEW

Taronga Park Zoo has occupied its superb waterfront location since 1916. The zoo is proud of its record for breeding endangered and rare species, and its collection of Australian animals, including Koalas in a treetop habitat, is comprehensive. Its exhibits allow the animals to live as naturally as possible while allowing visitors the chance to observe their behaviour. The zoo is the centre for many educational and entertaining activities and is the perfect city complement to Dubbo's Western Plains open-range zoo.

*Visitors to Taronga Park Zoo can enjoy seeing the animals and also a vista across Cremorne Point to the city centre.*

*Looking across the sandstone cliffs of North Head, with its national park, towards the Harbour entrance, South Head and the city.*

## NORTHERN BEACHES

There are two beaches at Manly, on either side of a slender neck of land. One beach faces the Harbour, the other fronts the rolling surf of the Pacific Ocean. Manly is only one of a chain of magnificent beaches which stretches up the coast from North Head, giving residents of Sydney's northern suburbs their own seaside playgrounds and attracting local and international holidaymakers.

*North of Sydney Harbour entrance is a chain of superb ocean beaches. Here, Barrenjoey Lighthouse, on Barrenjoey Headland, guards Palm Beach.*

*Manly's famous ocean beach braves the Pacific Ocean. This view extends south across Manly harbour beach to the Harbour and Sydney city.*

## SUN AND FRESH AIR ON THE CENTRAL COAST

The Central Coast, for many years a popular holiday destination, is fast becoming a dormitory suburb for Sydney. The coast's main city, Gosford, stands on Brisbane Water, a large expanse of water north of Broken Bay, and is accessible by freeway and rail from the northern suburbs of Sydney. Close to excellent surf beaches and national parks, the Central Coast also boasts the resorts of Terrigal, The Entrance and Toukley.

*Avoca Beach, one of the gems of the Central Coast of New South Wales, is within easy reach of Sydney.*

Top: Terrigal Beach is a well-known place to swim and enjoy the company of friends.

Above: The Entrance is north of Gosford, at the opening to Tuggerah Lakes.

*A lone angler tries his luck on Frazer Beach, Munmorah State Recreation Park, on the New South Wales Central Coast.*

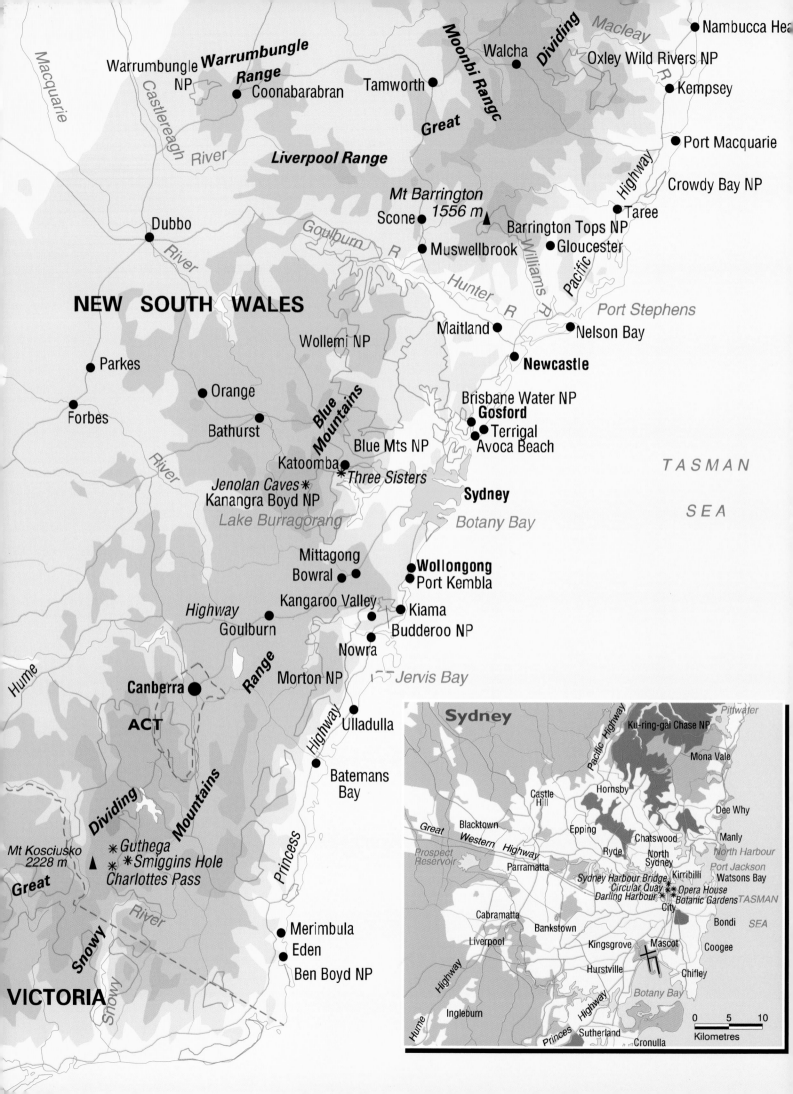

## SYDNEY – SURROUNDED BY NATURAL SPLENDOUR

Sydney surrounds Sydney Harbour then extends south to the coastal bushland of Royal National Park. Northwards its suburbs stretch through sandstone country and touch forested national parks on the way to the holidaymaker's paradise of the Central Coast. To the west, the Blue Mountains offer scenic bushland and spectacular mountain gorges.

This, the oldest city in Australia, was settled by British Marines, convicts and officials in 1788. The land on which it was established had been the province of indigenous people for many tens of thousands of years. They were forced to stand aside while a town was established and farms pushed out into the bush. In 1813, the crossing of the Blue Mountains allowed access for graziers and farmers to the rich lands beyond the Great Divide.

From Sydney, other major cities were founded, and today the city on the Harbour is Australia's oldest, largest and most active. It is a centre of commerce, culture and cuisine, the place where visitors to Australia are most likely to begin their pilgrimage Down Under, noted for its multiculturalism and yet a heartland of the Australian identity.

*Twilight bathes sky and water in flame that flickers on the sails of the Opera House.*

## INDEX